Weather Watchers

WET

WRITTEN BY
E.C. Andrews

KidHaven
PUBLISHING

Published in 2025 by
KidHaven Publishing, an Imprint of
Greenhaven Publishing, LLC
2544 Clinton St., Buffalo, NY 14224

Written by: E.C. Andrews
Edited by: Rebecca Phillips-Bartlett
Designed by: Ker Ker Lee

All facts, statistics, web addresses and URLs in this book were verified as valid and accurate at time of writing. No responsibility for any changes to external websites or references can be accepted by either the author or publisher.

Cataloging-in-Publication Data

Names: Andrews, E.C.
Title: Wet / E.C. Andrews.
Description: Buffalo, New York : KidHaven Publishing, 2025. | Series: Weather watchers | Includes glossary and index.
Identifiers: ISBN 9781534547438 (pbk.) | ISBN 9781534547445 (library bound) | ISBN 9781534547452 (ebook)
Subjects: LCSH: Precipitation (Meteorology)--Juvenile literature. | Rain and rainfall--Juvenile literature. | Weather--Juvenile literature.
Classification: LCC QC920.A537 2025 | DDC 551.57'7--dc23

Manufactured in the United States of America

CPSIA compliance information: Batch #CSKH25
For further information contact Greenhaven Publishing LLC at 1-844-317-7404.

Please visit our website, www.greenhavenpublishing.com.
For a free color catalog of all our high-quality books, call toll free 1-844-317-7404 or fax 1-844-317-7405.

IMAGE CREDITS

All images are courtesy of Shutterstock.com, unless otherwise specified. With thanks to Getty Images, Thinkstock Photo and iStockphoto.
Recurring – 32 pixels, ClassicVector, lineartestpilot, Net Vector, Macrovector. Cover – northallertonman, Brian A Jackson, Emagnetic, Barry Barnes, trendobjects. Character – Andrew Rybalko. 2–3 – LeManna. 4–5 – Evgeny Atamanenko, mykhailo pavlenko. 6–7 – worradirek, Julia Sudnitskaya. 8–9 – patpitchaya, vovan, Iqbal Rahmat ID. 10–11 – Moshbidon, forest pictures, Sudowoodo. 12–13 – Shiyari, New Africa. 14–15 – Bridget Zawitoski, 2M media, Gchapel . 16–17 – vvvita, IhorM. 18–19 – Makoto Ose, MariaLev, Smit. 20–21 – Derren, Marta Fernandez Jimenez, Sudowoodo, Perfect_kebab. 22–23 – Kichigin, KAMONRAT, Pogorelova Olga.

CONTENTS

Words that look like **this** can be found in the glossary on page 24.

WHAT IS WEATHER?

Thank you for tuning in to Weather Watchers TV. My name is Ella. I am speaking to you from under a very big umbrella right now. Why? Rainy weather, that's why!

The weather is what you see and feel when you go outside. Sometimes it is hot, sometimes it is cold. Sometimes, it is very, very WET. When was the last time you had wet weather?

WET WEATHER

Wet weather is caused by rain. Rain is when water droplets fall from the sky. Rain starts in clouds. Clouds are made of water. The water in the clouds grows into larger droplets over time.

The water droplets get larger and heavier. After a while, the water droplets get too heavy to stay in the air. They fall to the ground as rain.

WONDERFUL WATER

Look at those clouds! Rain is definitely on the way. Rain is one of the most important kinds of weather. A lot of animals, including humans, need rain for fresh drinking water.

Rain helps to feed plants and crops. Humans and animals need crops for food. Without rain, we would not have food. Rain helps to keep everything alive.

WET WEATHER SAFETY

Heavy rain can make it difficult to see. You should always be careful when crossing the road in wet weather. Rain can make the ground slippery. Walk carefully and use handrails where you can.

Rivers and lakes get deeper when it rains. This can make rivers flow much faster. Fast-flowing rivers can be dangerous if you fall in. Always keep a safe distance from deep, flowing water.

Monsoons

A monsoon is a strong wind that blows for many weeks and sometimes months. Monsoons happen in some areas of the world when the wind changes direction. Summer monsoons bring lots of rain. This is called a wet monsoon.

People in countries that have a lot of hot, dry weather need wet monsoons to survive. Without wet monsoons, they would not be able to grow food or have fresh water.

WET DISASTERS

Flooding can get very serious. Sometimes, people's streets and houses become flooded. But there are ways to stay safe. Water can only flow downwards, so moving to higher ground is a good idea.

Rain is not the only cause of floods. A tsunami is a big wave that crashes onto the shore when the ocean is pushed towards the land. Tsunamis are very dangerous and scary, but they are rare.

FREEZING RAIN

Water freezes when it reaches 32 degrees Fahrenheit (0 degrees Celsius). At this temperature, raindrops can freeze when they land. This makes an icy case around whatever the rain has landed on. It looks very beautiful.

Freezing rain can look pretty, but it can be dangerous. Freezing rain creates ice that is difficult to see. This can make roads and sidewalks very slippery. Be sure to walk carefully!

WET WEATHER WONDERS

Our eyes see sunlight as white, but it is actually made up of lots of different colors. When sunlight passes through a raindrop, the colors break off in different directions.

Once the colors have split into different directions, our eyes can see each color. This makes rainbows. Rainbows usually appear when sunlight peaks through clouds when it is raining.

WATERY WILDLIFE

Some animals love the rain. Wet weather is when aquatic animals such as frogs, otters, and ducks all come out to play. You might see more slugs and snails on the ground.

Slugs and snails cannot get too wet or too dry. They need to find a good balance between the two. The water in the air before and after rainfall is just right for them.

Slugs and snails can crawl much faster on wet surfaces.

HAPPY RAINY DAYS

A rainy day should never dampen your spirits. Rain makes so many beautiful things in nature. It plays a huge role in keeping our planet alive.

The next time it rains, do not be afraid to put on your coat and rain boots and go for a splash! Just keep the safety tips in mind. I am Ella. Thank you for tuning in to Weather Watchers TV.

GLOSSARY

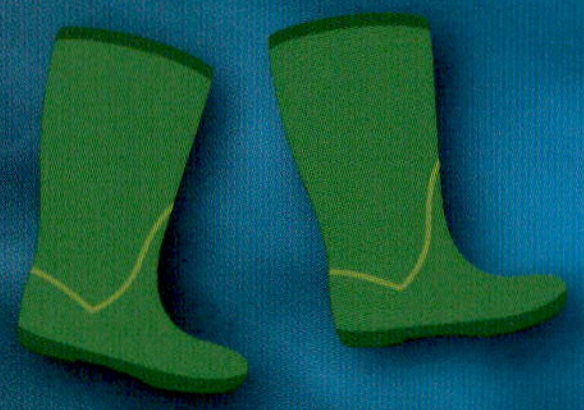

AQUATIC something where water plays an important role

BALANCE finding the right amount of something

CROPS plants that are grown on a large scale to be eaten or used

FAHRENHEIT a way of measuring temperature where water freezes at 32 degrees and boils at 212 degrees

HANDRAIL a rail used to grab onto so people do not slip or lose balance

SHORE where the ocean meets the land

TEMPERATURE how hot or cold something is

INDEX